To

_____

From

_____

Date

_____

The righteous man walks in his integrity;
His children are blessed after him.

—*Proverbs 20:7 NKJV*

FAMILY
CHRISTIAN
PRESS

Thank You to . . .
MY TEACHER

FAMILY CHRISTIAN PRESS
Grand Rapids, MI 49530

The quoted ideas expressed in this book (but not scripture verses) are not, in all cases, exact quotations, as some have been edited for clarity and brevity. In all cases, the author has attempted to maintain the speaker's original intent. In some cases, quoted material for this book was obtained from secondary sources, primarily print media. While every effort was made to ensure the accuracy of these sources, the accuracy cannot be guaranteed. For additions, deletions, corrections or clarifications in future editions of this text, please write FAMILY CHRISTIAN PRESS.

Cover Design by Colleen Boyle
Page Layout by Bart Dawson

ISBN 1-58334-355-5

Printed in the United States of America

Thank You to . . .
MY TEACHER

TABLE OF CONTENTS

Introduction

"Thank you, teacher!"—three words that have the power to warm the hearts and brighten the days of instructors everywhere. Because you're reading these words, it is likely that you are a teacher. If so, congratulations! You have chosen one of the world's most important professions. You've committed yourself to the noble cause of molding impressionable minds; by doing so, you are reshaping our schools and our future. This text is intended as a way of saying thanks.

Henry Adams correctly observed, "A teacher affects eternity; he can never tell where his influence stops." Those words have never been more true than they are today. We live in a difficult, fast-paced, temptation-filled world; more than ever, our young people need the leadership of godly mentors who are willing to teach by words and by example, but not necessarily in that order.

On the pages that follow, we consider topics of interest to Christians who teach. This book is intended to make you smile and to make you think. It contains Bible verses, quotations from noted Christian thinkers, and brief essays—all of which can lift your spirits and guide your path.

Whether you teach graduate school or Sunday School, whether you lecture at seminary or at Vacation Bible School, it's important to realize that God takes your teaching duties very seriously—and so should you. After all, you are God's emissary, a person charged with molding lives—it's a truly awesome responsibility.

So, if you are fortunate enough to find yourself in the role of teacher, accept a hearty congratulations and a profound word of thanks. And remember that God honors your profession just as surely as He offers His loving abundance to you and your students. With God's help, you are destined to reshape eternity. It's a big job, but don't worry—you and God, working together, can handle it.

Thank You for . . . Being a Teacher

Instruct and direct one another using good common sense.
And sing, sing your hearts out to God! Let every detail
in your lives—words, actions, whatever—
be done in the name of the Master, Jesus, thanking God
the Father every step of the way.

Colossians 3:16-17 MSG

Dear Teacher,

Thank you. Thanks for being someone we can look up to, and thanks for being someone we can learn from. Thanks for teaching us lessons from textbooks and lessons about life. Thank you for your concern, for your commitment, and for your encouragement.

Thanks for making our classes interesting (even when we're not very interested), and thanks for maintaining order in the classroom (even when we're not particularly orderly). Thank you for the lessons you taught, the papers you graded, the homework you corrected, and the time you invested after class. We know that your job is demanding, and we appreciate your dedication.

And finally, thanks for doing your part to make this world a better place. When you became a teacher, you did so because you wanted to help others; you have succeeded.

You have helped to shape our thoughts, and you have helped
to direct our lives. Because of you, we have learned and we
have grown. We will remember you always.

If a teacher fascinates with his doctrine,
his teaching never came from God.
The teacher who came from God is the one who clears
the way for Jesus and keeps it clear.

Oswald Chambers

It is desirable that children be kind,
appreciative and pleasant.
Those qualities should be taught and not hoped for.

James Dobson

WORDS OF WISDOM

If you want to be a teacher,
remember that you're just as likely to teach who you are
as you are to teach what you know.

Marie T. Freeman

No teacher should strive to make men think as he thinks,
but to lead them to the living Truth, to the Master himself,
of whom alone they can learn anything.

George MacDonald

Teaching is a divine calling. Whether we teach at home,
at church, or in a school classroom,
transfer of knowledge is a significant undertaking.

Suzanne Dale Ezell

Better to instruct a child than to collect riches.

Herve of Brittany

God often keeps us on the path by guiding us through
the counsel of friends and trusted spiritual advisors.

Bill Hybels

The next best thing to being wise oneself
is to live in a circle of those who are.

C. S. Lewis

The effective mentor strives to help a man or woman
discover what they can be in Christ and then holds them
accountable to become that person.

Howard Hendricks

WISDOM FROM GOD'S WORD

*My dear brothers and sisters, if anyone among you
wanders away from the truth and is brought back again,
you can be sure that the one who brings
that person back will save that sinner from death
and bring about the forgiveness of many sins.*

James 5:19-20 NLT

*Listen, my son, to your father's instruction
and do not forsake your mother's teaching.*

Proverbs 1:8 NIV

*A wise man will hear and increase learning,
and a man of understanding will attain wise counsel.*

Proverbs 1:5 NKJV

In every way be an example of doing good deeds.
When you teach, do it with honesty and seriousness.

Titus 2:7 NCV

The way of a fool is right in his own eyes,
but he who heeds counsel is wise.

Proverbs 12:15 NKJV

Acquire wisdom—how much better it is than gold!
And acquire understanding—it is preferable to silver.

Proverbs 16:16 HCSB

A TEACHER'S PRAYER

—————

Dear Lord, today I will celebrate the joys of teaching. Help me to be a cheerful, optimistic, encouraging teacher, today and every day.
Amen

Thank You for . . . Encouraging Excellence

*Let's see how inventive we can be in encouraging love
and helping out, not avoiding worshipping
together as some do but spurring each other on.*

Hebrews 10:24-25 MSG

Dear Teacher,

Thank you for setting high standards. Had you not done so, we would have suffered. If little is required of us, we often respond with minimum effort. But, because you demanded more, we gave more. And we learned as much from our hard work as we did from the textbooks we studied.

You taught us that excellence requires effort. And because you were willing to teach that lesson, we were compelled to learn it.

There was never a person who did anything worth doing that did not receive more than he gave.

Henry Ward Beecher

WORDS OF WISDOM

There is a canyon of difference between doing your best to
glorify God and doing whatever it takes to glorify yourself.
The quest for excellence is a mark of maturity.
The quest for power is childish.

Max Lucado

Few things fire up a person's commitment
like dedication to excellence.

John Maxwell

Excellence is not perfection, but essentially a desire
to be strong in the Lord and for the Lord.

Cynthia Heald

If, in your working hours, you make the work your end,
you will presently find yourself all unawares
inside the only circle in your profession that really matters.
You will be one of the sound craftsmen,
and other sound craftsmen will know it.

C. S. Lewis

Don't take hold of a thing unless you want
that thing to take hold of you.

E. Stanley Jones

If you want to achieve excellence, you can get there today.
As of this moment, quit doing less-than-excellent work.

Thomas J. Watson

Great relief and satisfaction can come from seeking
God's priorities for us in each season, discerning what is
"best" in the midst of many noble opportunities,
and pouring our most excellent energies into those things.

Beth Moore

A lot of people have gone further than they thought
they could because someone else thought they could.

Zig Ziglar

Encouraging others means helping people,
looking for the best in them,
and trying to bring out their positive qualities.

John Maxwell

WISDOM FROM GOD'S WORD

*You must warn each other every day,
as long as it is called "today," so that none of you will be
deceived by sin and hardened against God.*

Hebrews 3:13 NLT

*I want their hearts to be encouraged and joined together in
love, so that they may have all the riches
of assured understanding, and have the knowledge
of God's mystery—Christ.*

Colossians 2:2 HCSB

*Carry one another's burdens;
in this way you will fulfill the law of Christ.*

Galatians 6:2 HCSB

Anxiety in a man's heart weighs it down,
but a good word cheers it up.

Proverbs 12:25 HCSB

So then, we must pursue what promotes peace
and what builds up one another.

Romans 14:19 HCSB

Therefore encourage one another
and build each other up as you are already doing.

1 Thessalonians 5:11 HCSB

As iron sharpens iron, so people can improve each other.

Proverbs 27:17 NCV

A TEACHER'S PRAYER

*Dear Lord, I will strive to become
a teacher of dedication and skill.
Today, I will do my best,
and I will expect the best.
Amen*

Thank You for . . .
Lessons About Life

So teach us to number our days,
that we may gain a heart of wisdom.

Psalm 90:12 NKJV

Dear Teacher,

Thanks for the lessons about life. You have taught us about discipline, hope, courage, responsibility, and more.

One of life's great ironies is that there is so much to learn and so little time. That's why we value the lessons you have taught us. You cared enough to teach, and we won't forget.

The value of a life can only be estimated
by its relationship to God.

Oswald Chambers

WORDS OF WISDOM

You will find, as you look back upon your life, that
the moments when you have really lived are the moments
when you have done things in the spirit of love.

Henry Drummond

Jesus wants Life for us, Life with a capital L.

John Eldredge

Your life is not a boring stretch of highway.
It's a straight line to heaven. And just look at
the fields ripening along the way. Look at the tenacity
and endurance. Look at the grains of righteousness.
You'll have quite a crop at harvest . . . so don't give up!

Joni Eareckson Tada

One life is all we have, and we live it as we believe in living it. And then it is gone. But to sacrifice what you are and live without belief, that's more terrible than dying.

Joan of Arc

We are common earthenware jars, filled with the treasure of the riches of God. The jar is not important— the treasure is everything.

Corrie ten Boom

May you live all the days of your life.

Jonathan Swift

Life is simply hard. That's all there is to it.
Thank goodness, the intensity of difficulty rises and falls.
Some seasons are far more bearable than others,
but none is without challenge.

Beth Moore

As I contemplate all the sacrifices required in order
to live a life that is totally focused on Jesus Christ
and His eternal kingdom, the joy seeps out of my heart
onto my face in a smile of deep satisfaction.

Anne Graham Lotz

WISDOM FROM GOD'S WORD

And Jesus said unto them, I am the bread of life:
he that cometh to me shall never hunger;
and he that believeth on me shall never thirst.

John 6:35 KJV

He who follows righteousness and mercy finds life,
righteousness and honor.

Proverbs 21:21 NKJV

I am crucified with Christ: nevertheless I live; yet not I,
but Christ liveth in me: and the life which I now live in
the flesh I live by the faith of the Son of God, who loved me,
and gave himself for me.

Galatians 2:20 KJV

*Jesus saith unto him, I am the way, the truth, and the life:
no man cometh unto the Father, but by me.*

John 14:6 KJV

*Thou wilt show me the path of life: in thy presence is fulness
of joy; at thy right hand there are pleasures for evermore.*

Psalm 16:11 KJV

*Lord, tell me when the end will come and how long I will live.
Let me know how long I have. You have given me
only a short life . . . . Everyone's life is only a breath.*

Psalm 39:4-5 NCV

*I came so they can have real and eternal life,
more and better life than they ever dreamed of.*

John 10:10 MSG

A TEACHER'S PRAYER

———

*Lord, as I take the next steps on my life's
journey—whether at home or at school—
let me take them with You. You have promised
never to leave me or forsake me. You are always
with me, protecting me and encouraging me.
Whatever this day may bring,
I thank You for Your love and for Your strength.
Let me lean upon You, Father—
and trust You—this day and forever.
Amen*

Thank You for . . .
Your Wisdom

Buy the truth, and do not sell it,
also wisdom and instruction and understanding.

Proverbs 23:23 NKJV

Dear Teacher,

We have so much to learn—thank you for sharing your knowledge and your wisdom. You have helped us understand the value of education and the importance of lifetime learning. Sometimes, of course, we become tired of textbooks, tests, classrooms, and computer screens. But even when we would rather be anyplace other than school, you help us focus on the things we need to know. And because you're excited about learning, we become excited, too.

You have taught us that education is the tool by which we come to know and appreciate the world in which we live.

Nurture your mind with great thoughts.

Benjamin Disraeli

WORDS OF WISDOM

To know the will of God is the greatest knowledge!
To do the will of God is the greatest achievement.

George W. Truett

Knowledge is power.

Francis Bacon

A big difference exists between a head full of knowledge
and the words of God literally abiding in us.

Beth Moore

It's the things you learn after you know it all
that really count.

Vance Havner

A wise man makes more opportunities than he finds.

Francis Bacon

Wisdom is not wisdom when it is derived
from books alone.

Horace

The wise man gives proper appreciation in his life
to his past. He learns to sift the sawdust of heritage
in order to find the nuggets that make
the current moment have any meaning.

Grady Nutt

One can learn only by seeing one's mistakes.

C. S. Lewis

Wisdom is the right use of knowledge.
To know is not to be wise. Many men know a great deal,
and are all the greater fools for it. But to know how to use
knowledge is to have wisdom.

C. H. Spurgeon

God's plan for our guidance is for us to grow gradually
in wisdom before we get to the crossroads.

Bill Hybels

Wisdom takes us beyond the realm of mere right
and wrong. Wisdom takes into account our personalities,
our strengths, our weaknesses,
and even our present state of mind.

Charles Stanley

WISDOM FROM GOD'S WORD

*Now we see but a poor reflection as in a mirror;
then we shall see face to face. Now, I know in part;
then I shall know fully . . . .*

1 Corinthians 13:12 NIV

*If you need wisdom—if you want to know what
God wants you to do—ask him, and he will gladly tell you.
He will not resent your asking.*

James 1:5 NLT

*For this very reason, make every effort to supplement
your faith with goodness, goodness with knowledge,
knowledge with self-control, self-control with
endurance, endurance with godliness.*

2 Peter 1:5-6 HCSB

Wisdom is the principal thing; therefore get wisdom.
And in all your getting, get understanding.

Proverbs 4:7 NKJV

Give instruction to a wise man, and he will be still wiser;
Teach a just man, and he will increase in learning.

Proverbs 9:9 NKJV

A mocker seeks wisdom and doesn't find it,
but knowledge [comes] easily to the perceptive.

Proverbs 14:6 HCSB

The one who has contempt for instruction will pay the penalty,
but the one who respects a command will be rewarded.

Proverbs 13:13 HCSB

A TEACHER'S PRAYER

*Lord, You are my Teacher. Help me to be
a student of Your Word and a servant of
Your will. Let me live by the truth You reveal,
let me trust in the wisdom of
Your commandments, and let me teach others
the glory of Your ways.
Amen*

Thank You for . . . Encouraging Us to Behave Responsibly

Yes, my dear children, live in him so that when Christ comes back, we can be without fear and not be ashamed in his presence. If you know that Christ is all that is right, you know that all who do right are God's children.

1 John 2:28-29 NCV

Dear Teacher,

Sometimes we behaved irresponsibly; when we did, you taught us the error of our ways. You taught us that the greatest rewards in life are reserved for those of us who learn the art of self-discipline.

Doing the right thing is not always easy, especially when we're tired or frustrated. But, doing the wrong thing almost always leads to trouble, and sometimes, it leads to BIG trouble.

You taught us that behaving responsibly may be harder in the beginning, but that it's easier in the end. Thank you for that lesson. May we remember it always.

Whenever you do a thing,
act as if all the world were watching.

Thomas Jefferson

WORDS OF WISDOM

There is only one duty, only one safe course,
and that is to try to be right.

Winston Churchill

Action springs not from thought,
but from a readiness for responsibility.

Dietrich Bonhoeffer

Whether we know it or not, whether we agree
with it or not, whether we practice it or not, whether
we like it or not, we are accountable to one another.

Charles Stanley

God will take care of everything—the rest is up to you.

Lisa Whelchel

To know what people really think,
pay regard to what they do, rather than to what they say.

René Descartes

The first thing to do in examining the power
that dominates me is to take hold of the unwelcome fact
that I am responsible for being thus dominated.

Oswald Chambers

If you want to be respected for your actions,
then your behavior must be above reproach.

Rosa Parks

The evangelistic harvest is always urgent.
The destiny of men and of nations is always being decided.
Every generation is strategic. We are not responsible for
the past generation, and we cannot bear the full
responsibility for the next one, but we do have
our generation. God will hold us responsible
as to how well we fulfill our responsibilities
to this age and take advantage of our opportunities.

Billy Graham

Generally speaking, accountability is a willingness
to share our activities, conduct, and fulfillment
of assigned responsibilities with others.

Charles Stanley

WISDOM FROM GOD'S WORD

"Therefore I will judge you, O house of Israel,
every one according to his ways," says the Lord GOD.

Ezekiel 18:30 NKJV

You will show me the path of life;
in Your presence is fullness of joy;
at Your right hand are pleasures forevermore.

Psalm 16:11 NKJV

Let us not become weary in doing good,
for at the proper time we will reap a harvest
if we do not give up.

Galatians 6:9 NIV

So then each of us shall give account of himself to God.

Romans 14:12 NKJV

Now he who plants and he who waters are one,
and each one will receive his own reward
according to his own labor.

1 Corinthians 3:8 NKJV

But as God has distributed to each one,
as the Lord has called each one, so let him walk.

1 Corinthians 7:17 NKJV

A TEACHER'S PRAYER

———

*Lord, my students are both a priceless gift
and a profound responsibility. Let my actions
be worthy of that responsibility. Lead me along
Your path, Lord, and guide me far from
the frustrations and distractions of this troubled
world. Let Your Holy Word guide my actions,
and let Your love reside in my heart,
this day and every day.
Amen*

Thank You for . . . Being a Role Model

Stay at your post reading Scripture, giving counsel, teaching.
And that special gift of ministry you were given when
the leaders of the church laid hands on you and prayed—
keep that dusted off and in use. Cultivate these things.
Immerse yourself in them. The people will all see you mature
right before their eyes! Keep a firm grasp on both your
character and your teaching. Don't be diverted. Just keep at it.
Both you and those who hear you will experience salvation.

1 Timothy 4:13-16 MSG

Dear Teacher,

All of us need positive role models—thanks for being one. You have taught us some of life's most important lessons, not only by your words but also by your actions.

You weren't always perfect—nobody is—but when you did make mistakes, you corrected them, you moved on, and we learned.

Because of the example you've set, you are a powerful force for good inside the classroom and beyond . . . far beyond.

Be careful how you live.
You may be the only Bible some person ever reads.

William J. Toms

WORDS OF WISDOM

In our faith we follow in someone's steps.
In our faith we leave footprints to guide others.
It's the principle of discipleship.

Max Lucado

For one man who can introduce another to Jesus Christ
by the way he lives and by the atmosphere of his life,
there are a thousand who can only talk jargon about him.

Oswald Chambers

Living life with a consistent spiritual walk deeply
influences those we love most.

Vonette Bright

The lives of ministers oftentimes convince
more strongly than their words; their tongues
may persuade, but their lives command.

Thomas Brooks

Your life is destined to be an example.
The only question is "what kind?"

Marie T. Freeman

A man who lives right, and is right,
has more power in his silence
than another has by his words.

Phillips Brooks

We urgently need people who encourage
and inspire us to move toward God and away
from the world's enticing pleasures.

Jim Cymbala

Our walk counts far more than our talk, always!

George Mueller

Among the most joyful people I have known have been
some who seem to have had no human reason for joy.
The sweet fragrance of Christ has shown
through their lives.

Elisabeth Elliot

WISDOM FROM GOD'S WORD

*Because the kingdom of God is present
not in talk but in power.*

1 Corinthians 4:20 NCV

*We have around us many people whose lives tell us
what faith means. So let us run the race that is before us
and never give up. We should remove from our lives
anything that would get in the way
and the sin that so easily holds us back.*

Hebrews 12:1 NCV

*Do everything without grumbling and arguing,
so that you may be blameless and pure.*

Philippians 2:14-15 HCSB

Set an example of good works yourself,
with integrity and dignity in your teaching.

Titus 2:7 HCSB

I, therefore, the prisoner in the Lord,
urge you to walk worthy of the calling you have received.

Ephesians 4:1 HCSB

But whoever keeps His word, truly in him the love of God
is perfected. This is how we know we are in Him:
the one who says he remains in Him
should walk just as He walked.

1 John 2:5-6 HCSB

A TEACHER'S PRAYER

---

*Lord, let me be a righteous example
to my students. Let me be honest and good,
patient and kind, faithful to You
and loving to others . . . now and forever.
Amen*

Thank You for . . .
Listening

*My dear brothers and sisters, always be willing to listen
and slow to speak. Do not become angry easily,
because anger will not help you live
the right kind of life God wants.*

James 1:19-20 NCV

Dear Teacher,

Thanks for listening and for trying your best to understand. Sometimes, you must have been frustrated by the things that we said and did. But you listened anyway. And sometimes, you understood us far better than we understood ourselves.

You were willing to share your advice (which, regretfully, we often ignored), but you were also willing to let us make our own mistakes without saying, "I told you so."

Even when our words must have seemed silly or repetitive, you kept listening. And that made all the difference.

The cliché is true: People don't care what we know until they know we care.

Rick Warren

WORDS OF WISDOM

Listening is loving.

Zig Ziglar

Part of good communication is listening
with the eyes as well as with the ears.

Josh McDowell

One of the best ways to encourage someone
who's hurting is with your ears—by listening.

Barbara Johnson

Attitude and the spirit in which we communicate
are as important as the words we say.

Charles Stanley

Sleep not when others speak.

George Washington

Christian spirituality does not begin with us talking about
our experience; it begins with listening
to God call us, heal us, forgive us.

Eugene H. Peterson

When we come to Jesus stripped of pretensions,
with a needy spirit, ready to listen,
He meets us at the point of need.

Catherine Marshall

Listening, not imitation, is the sincerest form of flattery.

Joyce Brothers

I think the one lesson I have learned is that
there is no substitute for paying attention.

Diane Sawyer

We cannot experience the fullness of Christ
if we do all the expressing. We must allow God
to express His love, will, and truth to us.

Gary Smalley

Oh, I listen a lot and talk less.
You can't learn anything when you're talking.

Bing Crosby

WISDOM FROM GOD'S WORD

Answering before listening is both stupid and rude.

Proverbs 18:13 MSG

Listen carefully to wisdom; set your mind on understanding.

Proverbs 2:2 NCV

A wise man will listen and increase his learning,
and a discerning man will obtain guidance.

Proverbs 1:5 HCSB

A fool's way is right in his own eyes,
but whoever listens to counsel is wise.

Proverbs 12:15 HCSB

He awakens [Me] each morning; He awakens My ear to listen like those being instructed. The Lord GOD has opened My ear, and I was not rebellious; I did not turn back.

Isaiah 50:4-5 HCSB

You must follow the LORD your God and fear Him. You must keep His commands and listen to His voice; you must worship Him and remain faithful to Him.

Deuteronomy 13:4 HCSB

It is written in the Prophets: And they will all be taught by God. Everyone who has listened to and learned from the Father comes to Me.

John 6:45 HCSB

A TEACHER'S PRAYER

*Lord, give me the wisdom to be
a good listener. Help me listen carefully
to my family, to my friends, to my students,
and—most importantly—to You.
Amen*

Thank You for . . .
Teaching Us Discipline

No discipline seems pleasant at the time, but painful.
Later on, however, it produces a harvest of righteousness
and peace for those who have been trained by it.

Hebrews 12:11 NIV

Dear Teacher,

You are charged with a thankless task: controlling students who would prefer not to be controlled. Despite our wishes to the contrary, we need to be disciplined, and when we need discipline, you provide it.

You have taught us that orderly behavior is a prerequisite for success both inside and outside the classroom. Thank you. As we grow up, all of us learn powerful, life-changing lessons about the rewards of self-discipline. We are still learning. And you're still helping.

Work is doing it. Discipline is doing it every day.
Diligence is doing it well every day.

Dave Ramsey

WORDS OF WISDOM

As we seek to become disciples of Jesus Christ,
we should never forget that the word *disciple*
is directly related to the word *discipline*.
To be a disciple of the Lord Jesus Christ
is to know his discipline.

Dennis Swanberg

Diligence is the mother of good luck
and God gives all things to industry.

Ben Franklin

Self-discipline is an acquired asset.

Duke Ellington

Discipline is training that develops and corrects.

Charles Stanley

No sane man is unafraid in battle, but discipline produces
in him a form of vicarious courage.

George S. Patton

The alternative to discipline is disaster.

Vance Havner

In reading the lives of great men,
I found that the first victory they won was over themselves:
with all of them, self-discipline came first.

Harry S Truman

Your thoughts are the determining factor as to whose mold
you are conformed to. Control your thoughts
and you control the direction of your life.

Charles Stanley

How often it occurs to me, as it must to you,
that it is far easier simply to cooperate with God!

Beth Moore

A life lived in God is not lived on the plane of feelings,
but of the will.

Elisabeth Elliot

WISDOM FROM GOD'S WORD

I discipline my body and make it my slave.

1 Corinthians 9:27 NASB

Therefore by their fruits you will know them.

Matthew 7:20 NKJV

Whoever accepts correction is on the way to life,
but whoever ignores correction will lead others away from life.

Proverbs 10:17 NCV

But each person should examine his own work,
and then he will have a reason for boasting in himself alone,
and not in respect to someone else.
For each person will have to carry his own load.

Galatians 6:4-5 HCSB

You did not choose Me, but I chose you. I appointed you that you should go out and produce fruit, and that your fruit should remain, so that whatever you ask the Father in My name, He will give you.

John 15:16 HCSB

Run away from infantile indulgence. Run after mature righteousness—faith, love, peace—joining those who are in honest and serious prayer before God.

2 Timothy 2:22 MSG

Guide the young men to live disciplined lives. But mostly, show them all this by doing it yourself, incorruptible in your teaching, your words solid and sane.

Titus 2:6-8 MSG

A TEACHER'S PRAYER

*Dear Lord, Your Holy Word tells us that
You expect Your children to be diligent and
disciplined. You have told us that the fields are
ripe and the workers are few. Lead me to
Your fields, Lord, and make me a disciplined
teacher in the service of Your Son, Christ Jesus.
When I am weary, give me strength.
When I am discouraged, give me hope.
Make me a disciplined, courageous, industrious
servant for Your Kingdom today and forever.
Amen*

*Thank You for . . .
Teaching Truth*

*I have no greater joy than this,
to hear of my children walking in the truth.*

3 John 1:4 NASB

Dear Teacher,

Because you are in a position of leadership, you must ensure that the messages you share with your students are sound, practical, and true. The ultimate truth, of course, is found in the Word of God through the person of His Son Jesus. And even if Bible teachings are not a formal part of a school's curriculum, God's Word should be firmly planted in the heart of every Christian teacher.

Thank you for teaching the truth and for demonstrating it . . . but not necessarily in that order.

Truth walks by daylight, falsehood by night.

Raymond Lull

WORDS OF WISDOM

Truth will triumph. The Father of truth will win,
and the followers of truth will be saved.

Max Lucado

God offers to everyone the choice between truth
and repose. Take which you please,
but you can never have both.

Ralph Waldo Emerson

Let everything perish! Dismiss these empty vanities!
And let us take up the search for the truth.

St. Augustine

Learning God's truth and getting it into our heads
is one thing, but living God's truth and getting it
into our characters is quite something else.

Warren Wiersbe

Peace, if possible, but truth at any rate.

Martin Luther

The difficult truth about truth is that it often requires us
to change our perspectives, attitudes, and rules for living.

Susan Lenzkes

For Christians, God himself is the only absolute;
truth and ethics are rooted in his character.

Chuck Colson

Truth is always about something,
but reality is that about which truth is.

C. S. Lewis

Jesus differs from all other teachers;
they reach the ear, but he instructs the heart;
they deal with the outward letter,
but he imparts an inward taste for the truth.

C. H. Spurgeon

We have in Jesus Christ a perfect example
of how to put God's truth into practice.

Bill Bright

WISDOM FROM GOD'S WORD

These are the things you should do: Tell each other the truth.
In the courts judge with truth and complete fairness.

Zechariah 8:16 NCV

You will know the truth, and the truth will set you free.

John 8:32 HCSB

"You are a king then?" Pilate asked. "You say that I'm a king,"
Jesus replied. "I was born for this, and I have come into
the world for this: to testify to the truth.
Everyone who is of the truth listens to My voice."

John 18:37 HCSB

Be diligent to present yourself approved to God,
a worker who doesn't need to be ashamed,
correctly teaching the word of truth.

2 Timothy 2:15 HCSB

You have already heard about this hope in the message
of truth, the gospel that has come to you.
It is bearing fruit and growing all over the world,
just as it has among you since the day you heard it
and recognized God's grace in the truth.

Colossians 1:5-6 HCSB

A TEACHER'S PRAYER

*Heavenly Father, let me trust in Your Word
and in Your Son. Jesus said He was the truth,
and I believe Him. Make Jesus the standard
for truth in my life so that I might be a worthy
example to others and a worthy servant to You.
Amen*

Thank You for . . . Your Prayers

Be cheerful no matter what; pray all the time;
thank God no matter what happens.
This is the way God wants you who belong
to Christ Jesus to live.

1 Thessalonians 5:16-18 MSG

Dear Teacher,

If you said any prayers on our behalf, you did so for a very good reason: you knew how badly we needed them! God certainly heard your prayers, and we have certainly been blessed by them.

In today's uncertain world, all prayers are welcomed. Thanks for yours.

Two wings are necessary to lift our souls toward God:
prayer and praise. Prayer asks.
Praise accepts the answer.

Mrs. Charles E. Cowman

WORDS OF WISDOM

If I should neglect prayer but a single day,
I should lose a great deal of the fire of faith.

Martin Luther

Get into the habit of dealing with God about everything.

Oswald Chambers

I have been driven many times to my
knees by the overwhelming conviction that I had nowhere
else to go. My own wisdom, and that of all about me,
seemed insufficient for the day.

Abraham Lincoln

Are you weak? Weary? Confused? Troubled? Pressured?
How is your relationship with God? Is it held in its place
of priority? I believe the greater the pressure,
the greater your need for time alone with Him.

Kay Arthur

Just pray for a tough hide and a tender heart.

Ruth Bell Graham

When you affirm big, believe big,
and pray big, big things happen.

Norman Vincent Peale

To pray in the name of Jesus is not only to use
His name at the end of a prayer, but it is to pray
in the mind and in the spirit of Jesus.

R. A. Torrey

To pray is to mount on eagle's wings above the clouds
and get into the clear heaven where God dwells.

C. H. Spurgeon

Only that which lies outside the will of God
lies outside the reach of prayer.

R. G. Lee

WISDOM FROM GOD'S WORD

Let the words of my mouth and the meditation
of my heart be acceptable in Your sight,
O LORD, my strength and my Redeemer.

Psalm 19:14 NKJV

Let my prayer come before You; incline Your ear to my cry!

Psalm 88:2 NASB

Do not be anxious about anything, but in everything,
by prayer and petition, with thanksgiving,
present your requests to God.

Philippians 4:6 NIV

Rejoice in hope; be patient in affliction; be persistent in prayer.

Romans 12:12 HCSB

For the eyes of the LORD are over the righteous,
and his ears are open unto their prayers:
but the face of the LORD is against them that do evil.

1 Peter 3:12 KJV

Therefore I want the men in every place to pray,
lifting up holy hands without anger or argument.

1 Timothy 2:8 HCSB

A TEACHER'S PRAYER

*Dear Lord, when I pray, let me feel
Your presence. When I worship You,
let me feel Your love. In the quiet moments
of the day, I will open my heart to You,
Almighty God. And I know that You
are with me always and that
You will always hear my prayers.
Amen*

Thank You for . . . Helping Us Dream

*May the God of hope fill you with all joy
and peace as you trust in him, so that you may overflow
with hope by the power of the Holy Spirit.*

Romans 15:13 NIV

Dear Teacher,

Thanks for helping us dream. When we summoned the courage to confide in you, you supported us and you encouraged us. If you harbored any doubts, you hid them.

Your faith has encouraged us to expect big things from life and from ourselves. Now, it's up to each of us to transform our dreams into reality. Because of you and others like you, we will keep believing in the power of our dreams. And we will keep working until we make those dreams come true.

Always stay connected to people
and seek out things that bring you joy.
Dream with abandon. Pray confidently.

Barbara Johnson

WORDS OF WISDOM

To make your dream come true, you have to stay awake.

Dennis Swanberg

You cannot out-dream God.

John Eldredge

The future lies all before us. Shall it only be a slight
advance upon what we usually do?
Ought it not to be a bound, a leap forward to altitudes
of endeavor and success undreamed of before?

Annie Armstrong

Dreaming the dream of God is not for cowards.

Joey Johnson

Since it doesn't cost a dime to dream, you'll never
shortchange yourself when you stretch your imagination.

Robert Schuller

Allow your dreams a place in your prayers and plans.
God-given dreams can help you move into the future
He is preparing for you.

Barbara Johnson

You can look forward with hope, because one day
there will be no more separation, no more scars,
and no more suffering in My Father's House.
It's the home of your dreams!

Anne Graham Lotz

Every experience God gives us, every person
he brings into our lives, is the perfect preparation
for the future that only he can see.

Corrie ten Boom

Do not limit the limitless God! With Him,
face the future unafraid because you are never alone.

Mrs. Charles E. Cowman

You pay God a compliment by asking great things of Him.

St. Teresa of Avila

WISDOM FROM GOD'S WORD

Be of good courage, and he shall strengthen your heart,
all ye that hope in the LORD.

Psalm 31:24 KJV

When we have the opportunity to help anyone,
we should do it. But we should give special attention
to those who are in the family of believers.

Galatians 6:10 NCV

But if we hope for what we do not yet have,
we wait for it patiently.

Romans 8:25 NIV

*Looking at them, Jesus said, "With men it is impossible,
but not with God, because all things are possible with God."*

Mark 10:27 HCSB

Delayed hope makes the heart sick.

Proverbs 13:12 HCSB

*Let us hold on to the confession of our hope without wavering,
for He who promised is faithful.*

Hebrews 10:23 HCSB

*But as it is written: What no eye has seen and no ear
has heard, and what has never come into a man's heart,
is what God has prepared for those who love Him.*

1 Corinthians 2:9 HCSB

A TEACHER'S PRAYER

---

*Dear Lord, give me the courage to dream
and the wisdom to help my students do likewise.
When I am worried or weary, give me strength
for today and hope for tomorrow.
Keep me mindful of Your miraculous power,
Your infinite love, and Your eternal salvation.
Amen*

Thank You for . . .
Your Optimism

Make me hear joy and gladness.
Psalm 51:8 NKJV

Dear Teacher,

Thanks for sharing your optimistic spirit. You helped us believe in our hopes instead of our fears. When we fretted over the inevitable struggles of everyday living, you helped us regain perspective. When we worried about the uncertainty of tomorrow, you helped us focus on the opportunities of today.

Sometimes, of course, we will still fall prey to worry, frustration, anxiety, or sheer exhaustion. When we face life's inevitable challenges and disappointments, we will remember mentors like you, and we'll respond with courage, optimism, and perseverance.

I've never seen a monument erected to a pessimist.

Paul Harvey

WORDS OF WISDOM

We may run, walk, stumble, drive, or fly,
but let us never lose sight of the reason for the journey,
or miss a chance to see a rainbow on the way.

Gloria Gaither

The popular idea of faith is of a certain obstinate
optimism: the hope, tenaciously held in the face of trouble,
that the universe is fundamentally friendly
and things may get better.

J. I. Packer

The Christian lifestyle is not one of legalistic do's
and don'ts, but one that is positive, attractive, and joyful.

Vonette Bright

If you can't tell whether your glass is half-empty
or half-full, you don't need another glass; what you need
is better eyesight . . . and a more thankful heart.

Marie T. Freeman

At least ten times every day, affirm this thought:
"I expect the best and, with God's help,
I will attain the best."

Norman Vincent Peale

The people whom I have seen succeed best in life have
always been cheerful and hopeful people who went about
their business with a smile on their faces.

Charles Kingsley

Hope looks for the good in people, opens doors for people,
discovers what can be done to help, lights a candle,
does not yield to cynicism. Hope sets people free.

Barbara Johnson

The sun shines not on us, but in us.

John Muir

Christ can put a spring in your step and a thrill
in your heart. Optimism and cheerfulness
are products of knowing Christ.

Billy Graham

Don't miss the beautiful colors of the rainbow while
you're looking for the pot of gold at the end of it!

Barbara Johnson

WISDOM FROM GOD'S WORD

For God has not given us a spirit of fear,
but of power and of love and of a sound mind.

2 Timothy 1:7 NLT

I can do everything through him that gives me strength.

Philippians 4:13 NIV

My cup runs over. Surely goodness and mercy
shall follow me all the days of my life;
and I will dwell in the house of the LORD Forever.

Psalm 23:5-6 NKJV

Is anything impossible for the LORD?

Genesis 18:14 HCSB

But Jesus looked at them and said to them,
"With men this is impossible,
but with God all things are possible."

Matthew 19:26 NKJV

But as it is written: "Eye has not seen, nor ear heard,
nor have entered into the heart of man the things which
God has prepared for those who love Him."

1 Corinthians 2:9 NKJV

But if we hope for what we do not see,
we eagerly wait for it with patience.

Romans 8:25 HCSB

A TEACHER'S PRAYER

Lord, give me faith, optimism, and hope.
Let me expect the best from You,
and let me look for the best in my students.
Let me trust You, Lord, to direct my life.
And, let me be Your faithful, hopeful,
optimistic servant every day that I live.
Amen

Thank You for . . .
Your Courage

So we may boldly say: "The Lord is my helper;
I will not fear. What can man do to me?"

Hebrews 13:6 NKJV

Dear Teacher,

In difficult times, we learn lessons that we could have learned in no other way: We learn about life, but more importantly, we learn about ourselves. Thank you for teaching us to live courageously.

Every human life, like every teaching career, is a tapestry of events: some grand, some not-so-grand, and some downright disappointing. You showed us that our disappointments and failures should never be considered "final" if we possess the courage to face our mistakes and the wisdom to learn from them.

Courage is contagious.

Billy Graham

WORDS OF WISDOM

Courage is the price that life exacts for granting peace.
The soul that knows it not knows
no release from little things.

Amelia Earhart

One man with courage makes a majority.

Andrew Jackson

Our Lord is searching for people who will
make a difference. Christians dare not dissolve
into the background or blend into
the neutral scenery of the world.

Charles Swindoll

With each new experience of letting God be in control,
we gain courage and reinforcement
for daring to do it again and again.

Gloria Gaither

Just as courage is faith in good, so discouragement is
faith in evil, and, while courage opens the door to good,
discouragement opens it to evil.

Hannah Whitall Smith

Are you fearful? First, bow your head
and pray for God's strength. Then, raise your head
knowing that, together, you and God can handle
whatever comes your way.

Jim Gallery

Success is not measured by what a man accomplishes,
but by the opposition he has encountered,
and the courage with which he maintained
the struggle against overwhelming odds.

Charles A. Lindbergh, Jr.

You gain strength, courage and confidence
every time you look fear in the face.

Eleanor Roosevelt

There comes a time when we simply have to face
the challenges in our lives and stop backing down.

John Eldredge

WISDOM FROM GOD'S WORD

God doesn't want us to be shy with his gifts,
but bold and loving and sensible.

2 Timothy 1:7 MSG

But when Jesus heard it, He answered him,
"Don't be afraid. Only believe."

Luke 8:50 HCSB

But He said to them, "Why are you fearful, you of little faith?"
Then He got up and rebuked the winds and the sea.
And there was a great calm.

Matthew 8:26 HCSB

Haven't I commanded you: be strong and courageous?
Do not be afraid or discouraged,
for the LORD your God is with you wherever you go.

Joshua 1:9 HCSB

The LORD is the One who will go before you.
He will be with you; He will not leave you or forsake you.
Do not be afraid or discouraged.

Deuteronomy 31:8 HCSB

A TEACHER'S PRAYER

*Lord, sometimes, this world is a fearful place
for my students and for me. Yet, You have
promised that You are with us always.
Today, Dear Lord, I will live courageously,
and I will encourage others to be strong.
I will place my trust in You
today, tomorrow, and forever.
Amen*

Thank You for . . .
Your Faith

For whatever is born of God overcomes the world.
And this is the victory that has
overcome the world—our faith.

1 John 5:4 NKJV

Dear Teacher,

Life demands faith and lots of it. But sometimes, faith is in short supply, especially when we encounter circumstances that leave us discouraged or afraid. As young people living in a difficult age, we need faith in the future, faith in ourselves, and faith in our Creator.

All of us must suffer through times of disappointment and doubt. When our own faith waned, you willingly shared yours. For that, we will be forever grateful.

Faith means believing in advance
what will only make sense in reverse.

Philip Yancey

WORDS OF WISDOM

God delights to meet the faith of one who looks up
to Him and says, "Lord, You know that I cannot do this—
but I believe that You can!"

Amy Carmichael

Faith based on experience is not faith; faith based
on God's revealed truth is the only faith there is.

Oswald Chambers

Do something that demonstrates faith,
for faith with no effort is no faith at all.

Max Lucado

Faith means you want God and want to want nothing else.

Brennan Manning

Just as our faith strengthens our prayer life,
so do our prayers deepen our faith. Let us pray often,
starting today, for a deeper, more powerful faith.

Shirley Dobson

Faith in God will not get for you everything you want,
but it will get for you what God wants you to have.
The unbeliever does not need what he wants;
the Christian should want only what he needs.

Vance Havner

How do you walk in faith? By claiming the promises of
God and obeying the Word of God, in spite of what
you see, how you feel, or what may happen.

Warren Wiersbe

I am truly grateful that faith enables me
to move past the question of "Why?"

Zig Ziglar

Faith is seeing light with the eyes of your heart,
when the eyes of your body see only darkness.

Barbara Johnson

Faith is not belief without proof,
but trust without reservation.

Elton Trueblood

WISDOM FROM GOD'S WORD

We live by faith, not by sight.

2 Corinthians 5:7 NIV

*The fundamental fact of existence is that this trust in God,
this faith, is the firm foundation under
everything that makes life worth living.*

Hebrews 11:1 MSG

*If you do not stand firm in your faith,
then you will not stand at all.*

Isaiah 7:9 HCSB

Be alert, stand firm in the faith, be brave and strong.

1 Corinthians 16:13 HCSB

*Now without faith it is impossible to please God,
for the one who draws near to Him must believe
that He exists and rewards those who seek Him.*

Hebrews 11:6 HCSB

*I have fought a good fight, I have finished my course,
I have kept the faith.*

2 Timothy 4:7 KJV

Is anything too hard for the LORD?

Genesis 18:14 KJV

A TEACHER'S PRAYER

*Dear Lord, help me to be a teacher
whose faith is strong and whose heart is pure.
Help me to remember that You are always near
and that You can overcome any challenge.
With Your love and Your power, Lord,
I can live courageously and faithfully
today and every day.
Amen*

Thank You for . . .
Your Kindness

*Be kind to each other, tenderhearted, forgiving one another,
just as God through Christ has forgiven you.*

Ephesians 4:32 NLT

Dear Teacher,

Amid the stressful moments of your demanding days, you slowed down long enough to sow seeds of kindness. And we noticed.

You are generous with your time and your praise. You are quick to share a thoughtful word, a genuine smile, or a helping hand. Through your words and your deeds, you demonstrate the power of compassion. May God bless you always, just as you have blessed us.

When you launch an act of kindness
out into the crosswinds of life,
it will blow kindness back to you.

Dennis Swanberg

WORDS OF WISDOM

It is one of the most beautiful compensations of life
that no one can sincerely try to help another
without helping herself.

Barbara Johnson

Goodness is the only investment that never fails.

Henry David Thoreau

Always be a little kinder than necessary.

James Barrie

When you extend hospitality to others, you're not trying
to impress people, you're trying to reflect God to them.

Max Lucado

I choose gentleness. Nothing is won by force.
I choose to be gentle. If I raise my voice may it be only
in praise. If I clench my fist, may it be only in prayer.
If I make a demand, may it be only of myself.

Max Lucado

I can usually sense that a leading is from the Holy Spirit
when it calls me to humble myself, serve somebody,
encourage somebody or give something away.
Very rarely will the evil one lead us to do
those kind of things.

Bill Hybels

Carve your name on hearts, not on marble.

C. H. Spurgeon

There are times when we are called to love,
expecting nothing in return. There are times when we are
called to give money to people who will never say thanks,
to forgive those who won't forgive us, to come early
and stay late when no one else notices.

Max Lucado

Constant kindness can accomplish much.
As the sun makes ice melt, kindness causes
misunderstanding, mistrust and hostility to evaporate.

Albert Schweitzer

WISDOM FROM GOD'S WORD

*Carry each other's burdens, and in this way you will
fulfill the law of Christ.*

Galatians 6:2 NIV

*Talk and act like a person expecting to be judged by
the Rule that sets us free. For if you refuse to act kindly,
you can hardly expect to be treated kindly.
Kind mercy wins over harsh judgment every time.*

James 2:12-13 MSG

*Finally, all of you be of one mind, having compassion for one
another; love as brothers, be tenderhearted, be courteous.*

1 Peter 3:8 NKJV

*And may the Lord make you increase
and abound in love to one another and to all.*

1 Thessalonians 3:12 NKJV

Just as you want others to do for you, do the same for them.

Luke 6:31 HCSB

*Be kindly affectionate to one another with brotherly love,
in honor giving preference to one another; not lagging in
diligence, fervent in spirit, serving the Lord; rejoicing in hope,
patient in tribulation, continuing steadfastly in prayer.*

Romans 12:10-12 NKJV

A TEACHER'S PRAYER

Lord, make me a loving, encouraging Christian.
And, let my love for Christ be reflected through
the kindness that I show to my students,
to my family, to my friends, and to all
who need the healing touch
of the Master's hand.
Amen

Thank You for . . .
Your Encouragement

But encourage each other every day while it is "today."
Help each other so none of you will
become hardened because sin has tricked you.

Hebrews 3:13 NCV

Dear Teacher,

Thank you for your encouragement. Even when we did not believe in ourselves, you believed in us . . . and it showed.

Life is a team sport, and all of us need occasional pats on the back from our parents, our friends, and our teachers. As a thoughtful teacher, you know that encouragement is a powerful tool for shaping the minds and hearts of your students. Thankfully, you never gave up on us, and you never stopped believing in our abilities—and because you believed, so, too, did we.

_____

How many people stop because so few say, "Go!"

Charles Swindoll

WORDS OF WISDOM

If your experiences would benefit anybody,
give them to someone.

Florence Nightingale

Isn't it funny the way some combinations of words
can give you—almost apart from their meaning—
a thrill like music?

C. S. Lewis

One of the ways God refills us after failure is through
the blessing of Christian fellowship. Just experiencing
the joy of simple activities shared with other children
of God can have a healing effect on us.

Anne Graham Lotz

We can never untangle all the woes in other people's lives.
We can't produce miracles overnight.
But we can bring a cup of cool water to a thirsty soul,
or a scoop of laughter to a lonely heart.

Barbara Johnson

Great people are those who make others feel
that they, too, can become great.

Mark Twain

A single word, if spoken in a friendly spirit, may be
sufficient to turn one from dangerous error.

Fanny Crosby

Invest in the human soul.
Who knows, it might be a diamond in the rough.

Mary McLeod Bethune

Encouragement is the oxygen of the soul.

John Maxwell

Kind words do not cost much. Although they cost little,
they accomplish much. Kind words produce
a beautiful image on men's souls.

Pascal

To the loved, a word of affection is a morsel,
but to the love-starved, a word of affection can be a feast.

Max Lucado

WISDOM FROM GOD'S WORD

Bear one another's burdens, and so fulfill the law of Christ.

Galatians 6:2 NKJV

As iron sharpens iron, so people can improve each other.

Proverbs 27:17 NCV

*I want their hearts to be encouraged and joined
together in love, so that they may have all the riches
of assured understanding, and have the knowledge
of God's mystery—Christ.*

Colossians 2:2 HCSB

*And let us be concerned about one another in order
to promote love and good works.*

Hebrews 10:24 HCSB

*Anxiety in a man's heart weighs it down,
but a good word cheers it up.*

Proverbs 12:25 HCSB

*So then, we must pursue what promotes peace
and what builds up one another.*

Romans 14:19 HCSB

A TEACHER'S PRAYER

*Dear Father, make me an encouraging teacher.
Just as You have lifted me up, let me also
lift up my students in the spirit of encouragement
and hope. Today, let me help my students find
the strength and the courage to use their gifts
according to Your master plan.
Amen*

Thank You for . . .
Your Patience
and Perseverance

Be gentle to all, able to teach, patient.
2 Timothy 2:24 NKJV

Dear Teacher,

We know that teaching requires patience—lots of patience—because the classroom can be a frustrating place. But you never allowed the inevitable frustrations of life here at school to overwhelm you.

When we made a mess of things, you disciplined us, you forgave us, and you convinced us that we could make amends.

You maintained your composure even when we didn't. When you demonstrated the power of patience, we watched, we listened, and we learned an important lesson. Thank you.

Genius is nothing more than
a greater aptitude for patience.

Ben Franklin

WORDS OF WISDOM

Let God use times of waiting to mold and shape
your character. Let God use those times to purify your life
and make you into a clean vessel for His service.

Henry Blackaby and Claude King

The challenge before us is to have faith in God,
and the hardest part of faith is waiting.

Jim Cymbala

The times we find ourselves having to wait on others
may be the perfect opportunities to train ourselves
to wait on the Lord.

Joni Eareckson Tada

If only we could be as patient with other people
as God is with us!

Jim Gallery

There is more to life than increasing its speed.

Gandhi

Waiting means going about our assigned tasks,
confident that God will provide the meaning
and the conclusions.

Eugene Peterson

The best thing one can do when it is raining
is to let it rain.

Henry Wadsworth Longfellow

If you want to hear God's voice clearly and you are
uncertain, then remain in His presence until He changes
that uncertainty. Often much can happen during this
waiting for the Lord. Sometimes He changes pride into
humility; doubt into faith and peace . . . .

Corrie ten Boom

The strongest of all warriors are these two:
time and patience.

Leo Tolstoy

You can't step in front of God and not get in trouble.
When He says, "Go three steps," don't go four.

Charles Stanley

WISDOM FROM GOD'S WORD

Patience is better than pride.

Ecclesiastes 7:8 NLT

Yet the LORD longs to be gracious to you;
he rises to show you compassion. For the LORD is a God
of justice. Blessed are all who wait for him!

Isaiah 30:18 NIV

Rejoice in hope; be patient in affliction; be persistent in prayer.

Romans 12:12 HCSB

Love is patient; love is kind.

1 Corinthians 13:4 HCSB

Now we exhort you, brethren, warn those who are unruly,
comfort the fainthearted, uphold the weak,
be patient with all.

1 Thessalonians 5:14 NKJV

But if we hope for what we do not see,
we eagerly wait for it with patience.

Romans 8:25 HCSB

I waited patiently for the LORD;
And He inclined to me, And heard my cry.

Psalm 40:1 NKJV

A TEACHER'S PRAYER

*Make me a patient teacher, Lord,
slow to anger and quick to forgive.
When I am hurried, slow me down.
When I become impatient with others,
give me empathy. Today, let me be
a patient servant as I trust in You,
Father, and in Your master plan.
Amen*

Thank You for . . .
Your Enthusiasm

Whatever you do, work at it with all your heart,
as working for the Lord, not for men.

Colossians 3:23 NIV

Dear Teacher,

Thank you for your enthusiasm. A teacher's attitude affects the mood of the entire classroom, and your enthusiasm is contagious. Because you are upbeat and enthusiastic, you make it easy to learn.

Mary Kay Ash once observed, "A mediocre idea that generates enthusiasm will go farther than a great idea that inspires no one." Because you have inspired us, we will carry your great ideas with us wherever we go.

God commands us to be filled with the Spirit,
and if we are not filled,
it is because we are living beneath our privileges.

D. L. Moody

WORDS OF WISDOM

We act as though comfort and luxury were the chief
requirements of life, when all we need to make us really
happy is something to be enthusiastic about.

Charles Kingsley

Each day, look for a kernel of excitement.

Barbara Jordan

There seems to be a chilling fear of holy enthusiasm among
the people of God. We try to tell how happy we are—
but we remain so well-controlled that there are very few
waves of glory experienced in our midst.

A. W. Tozer

Enthusiasm, like the flu, is contagious—
we get it from one another.

Barbara Johnson

Flaming enthusiasm, backed by horse sense
and persistence, is the quality that most frequently
makes for success.

Dale Carnegie

Don't take hold of a thing unless you want
that thing to take hold of you.

E. Stanley Jones

Think enthusiastically about everything,
especially your work.

Norman Vincent Peale

When we wholeheartedly commit ourselves to God,
there is nothing mediocre or run-of-the-mill about us.
To live for Christ is to be passionate about
our Lord and about our lives.

Jim Gallery

Catch on fire with enthusiasm and people will come
for miles to watch you burn.

John Wesley

Success is going from failure to failure
without loss of enthusiasm.

Winston Churchill

Some of us simmer all our lives and never come to a boil.

Vance Havner

WISDOM FROM GOD'S WORD

Never be lazy in your work,
but serve the Lord enthusiastically.

Romans 12:11 NLT

Be strong and brave, and do the work.
Don't be afraid or discouraged, because the Lord God,
my God, is with you. He will not fail you or leave you.

1 Chronicles 28:20 NCV

I have seen that there is nothing better than for a person
to enjoy his activities, because that is his reward.
For who can enable him to see what will happen after he dies?

Ecclesiastes 3:22 HCSB

He did it with all his heart. So he prospered.

2 Chronicles 31:21 NKJV

I have spoken these things to you so that
My joy may be in you and your joy may be complete.

John 15:11 HCSB

Rejoice in the Lord always. I will say it again: Rejoice!

Philippians 4:4 HCSB

Delight yourself also in the LORD,
and He shall give you the desires of your heart.

Psalm 37:4 NKJV

A TEACHER'S PRAYER

*Lord, when the classroom leaves me exhausted,
let me turn to You for strength and for renewal.
When I follow Your will for my life, You will
renew my enthusiasm. Let Your will be my will,
Lord, and let me find my strength in You.*
Amen